MOLLY BROWN
Denver's Unsinkable Lady

By
Christine Whitacre

*With Foreword by Tammy Grimes
and Introduction by Debbie Reynolds*

Fourth Printing, July 1997

This publication was made possible in part through grants from the McGraw-Hill Foundation and the Adolph Coors Foundation.

© Copyright 1984, Historic Denver, Inc.

Library of Congress Catalog Number: 84-081286

International Standard Book Number: 0-914248-03-0

Printed in the United States of America

Published by Historic Denver, Inc.

Cover design by Peter Hesse.

Historic Denver, Inc. is a non-profit, private organization first created in 1970 to restore Molly Brown's Victorian residence. Today, as a community advocate for saving Denver's past, members promote preservation throughout the city. Historic Denver has a professional staff of preservation, architectural and museum specialists. Historic Denver continues to be a resource for keeping Denver's architectural heritage and enriching the quality of life of the city.

Foreword

Many miracles occur every day to all of us alive. I expect in my lifetime that playing Molly Brown in the musical **The Unsinkable Molly Brown** (or as my daughter who was four years old at that time called it "The Unthinkable Molly Brown") was a miracle for me. It was the divine moment when out of all the hurly-burly of putting such a vehicle on its feet, Miss Brown and I came together as one person, and we both as one, sailed to stardom within the hearts of the American people and all who saw her — even when Grimes "spoke too fast."

After playing her 1,800 times from New York City to Denver, to the West Coast, back to our final show in Boston, I considered Molly Brown and Tammy Grimes to be **mine** forever. The spirit of Molly is forever remembered by the faces wreathed in smiles of those who come up to me everywhere I go in this world, who tell me, "I remember you in?...about the little girl who — Molly, yes, Molly Brown."

Perhaps Meredith Willson knew before we had opened he'd written the ultimate Broadway heroine's song for the American Public. I sure as hell didn't, but I sure as hell do **now**.

Tammy Grimes

Tammy Grimes

Introduction

Having been born in Texas and raised in California, I had never heard of Colorado's famous lady, Molly Brown.

My first meeting with her was seeing the Broadway production of **The Unsinkable Molly Brown.** *I fell in love then but never dared to dream I would be asked to do the film. When that happened, I really began studying and delving into the history of Molly Brown.*

As I did I found myself experiencing a knowledge not only of Molly and her Johnny's life, but a true feeling of warmth and excitement about Leadville and Denver, Colorado!

To me Molly was a female ahead of her time. Today she would be called a feminist, an independent woman who believed in growth and self expression. She was going to learn to read n' write — to go n' see — to be what she had to be — even to make mistakes.

Her Johnny, known as J.J. long before the television series **Dallas** *made initials famous, loved her as he loved his mountains. He just never was completely happy away from what he called God's beauty and simple people.*

That Mr. and Mrs. Brown were not adopted by early Denver society was somewhat understandable. They were nonconformists, very colorful, young, honest, very rich and unusual. But they helped color a wonderful city. And I am certain part of their big hearts and excitement are part of Denver's warmth, openness and generous giving today and always will be.

I loved making the film **The Unsinkable Molly Brown***. When an actress learns something important from the interpretations of an exciting, historical character, it remains with her always. As a woman, it was to learn to fight for higher and better goals in life and always try to be "unsinkable."*

I was honored by being nominated for an Academy Award for my portrayal of Molly. I only wish I had won it for her sake. But perhaps Molly knows the belief in the film industry — the accolade is to be chosen at all by one's peers.

Being Molly for even the six months it took to make the film meant so much to me that I bought a small piece of her Colorado, close to Leadville and Denver (actually a location of the film). There I built a home where each year my parents live from May to October. I go there as often as possible to enjoy the wonder, beauty and serenity of J.J.'s mountains and give myself a spiritual treat. I also visit Molly's home in Denver, I pray Denver will always keep that part of her colorful past open to the public.

I want to thank Historic Denver, Inc., for allowing me to be a tiny part of this book.

And thank you Molly Brown for being you! You must have had great fun and joy in life. I had and always will retain the joy of playing and knowing you.

Debbie Reynolds

Photo courtesy Denver Public Library, Western History Department.

Margaret Tobin Brown

Maggie Brown was once asked why she allowed all those wild stories about her to circulate. There was, for example, the story of her childhood when, floating down the Mississippi River on a raft, she was capsized by a cyclone and rescued by Mark Twain — the same Mark Twain who would later tell her to move west. There was also the tale of how after her husband J.J. hit "pay dirt" in the Little Jonny Mine, the floors of their Leadville home were inlaid with silver dollars. The accounts of her heroism on the *Titanic* became more fantastic with every telling. And, of course, there is the story of the potbelly stove. One day, the legend goes, when she and her husband James Joseph Brown were living in their cabin outside Leadville, J.J. brought home a $300,000 mining payroll. His young wife put it in the stove for safe-keeping and when J.J. came home that night, chilled by the cool mountain air, he lit the stove and the fortune was lost. The amount of money in that story, *if* there's any truth to it, would have been closer to $75.

"You know that story isn't true," her cousin Dolly Brown charged about the potbelly stove tale, "why do you let them keep telling it?" "It's a damn good story," Maggie replied. "And I don't care what the newspapers say about me, just so they say something."

Indeed, it is difficult to separate fact from fiction in Margaret Tobin Brown's life. Even her name has been fictionalized. The "Unsinkable Molly" was not called Molly in her lifetime. But Maggie loved publicity and her active imagination and theatrical flair helped perpetuate such stories. They became more exaggerated after her death. And the 1960s Broadway musical and Hollywood movie that glamorized her life — even if they did gloss over her considerable personal difficulties — finally succeeded in making her name a household word.

But Maggie Brown's life did not have to be fictionalized to be made interesting. She *was* a remarkable woman, and her life was touched by several major events of the late 1800s and early 1900s: the Gold Rush to the West, the rags-to-riches transformations that shaped a national consciousness, the tragedy of the *Titanic*, the social climbing of *nouveau riche*, and the lifestyle enjoyed by millionaires in America's "Gilded Age." These stories captured the imagination of Maggie's generation, and ours today.

Life on the Broadax Trail*

Margaret Tobin was born July 18, 1867, in Hannibal, Missouri. It was a town made famous by Samuel Langhorne Clemens, better known as Mark Twain. Years later, when she was a national celebrity, Maggie visited her hometown for the dedication of a Mark Twain memorial. While there, she alluded to her family's friendship with the famous author and made no effort to stem rumors that Twain and her father were boyhood pals. The stories were false, however. Twain was establishing himself as a writer and lecturer the year Maggie was born; and Maggie's father, John, was an uneducated, Irish-born widower with one child by the time he reached Hannibal.

John Tobin was born in Ireland in 1823. As a boy, he immigrated to the U.S.A. with an uncle. In Charleston, Virginia, Tobin married Catherine Pickett. When Catherine died a few years later, Tobin and their young daughter, Katie, continued the journey west, finally settling in Hannibal. Here, he married Johanna Collins, also an Irish immigrant and a widow with one daughter, Mary Ann. Johanna would bear John four more children: Daniel in 1863, Margaret in 1867, William in 1869, and Helen — often called Ellen — in 1871.

John Tobin was 40 years old when he started his second family and, as a laborer at the Hannibal Gas Works, he struggled to support his wife and children. Still, he was able to buy his own home, a tiny frame house located at the corner of Denkler Alley and Butler Street just a few blocks away from the Mississippi River. The home, now restored by the Marion County Historical Society, is composed of one bedroom, a kitchen, a "front room," and a basement room dug into the side of a hill.

*This and the next chapter heading were taken from an autobiography which Maggie planned to write, a venture which apparently never progressed past the chapter headings.

The Tobin family home in Hannibal, Missouri, consisted of a basement room, a bedroom, a kitchen, and a "front room." *Photo courtesy Denver Public Library, Western History Department.*

Although the Tobin children attended grammar school (dispelling later myths that Maggie was uneducated and unable to read and write at the time she became wealthy), the family's financial condition, and certainly their cramped living quarters, encouraged the children to either marry or go to work. By the time Maggie finished school at 13, her half-sisters Katie, 24, and Mary Ann, 23, were married. Brother Daniel sold newspapers on railroad cars, and Maggie soon found work in Garth's Tobacco Factory. Later, she worked as a waitress in at least one of the town's hotels.

It was while working as a waitress that Maggie, reportedly, met Mark Twain, who told her about the adventures and fortunes to be found in the West. It is possible Maggie met the famous author at this time, as Twain loved Hannibal and visited it often during these years. More likely, however, it was Twain's books — and the advice of Horace Greeley — that turned Maggie's thoughts westward.

Since the Pikes Peak Gold Rush of 1859, popular magazines and newspapers had romanticized life in Colorado. Here, the popular pulp declared, fortunes lay waiting for the taking. And though the vast majority of fortune-hunters found disappointment, enough *bona fide* success stories did exist to keep the dreamers coming.

All Roads Lead to Leadville

In 1876, the Gallagher brothers — John, Charles and Patrick — arrived in Leadville, Colorado. With virtually no background in mining, they started digging, struck silver, and when they sold their property to the St. Louis Smelting and Refining Company in the winter of 1877-78, the price was $225,000. Stories like that captured the imagination of the nation.

And, certainly, the imagination of some "shanty Irish" youngsters in Hannibal, Missouri.

In 1883, Maggie's half-sister Mary Ann and her husband Jack Landrigan moved to Leadville. Three years later, Maggie and Daniel followed. The journey, Maggie would later say, was made in a prairie schooner caravan that was waylaid and

Young Maggie worked as a clerk in Leadville's Daniels, Fisher & Smith dry goods store. She later claimed she spent her evenings starring in her own "penny shows," regaling miners with poetry recitals and songs. During each performance she surveyed the audience in search of a rich husband. *Photo courtesy Colorado Historical Society.*

robbed by Jesse James, providing her with a closeup look at that adventurer.

In fact, the railroad had been in Leadville since 1880 and Maggie and Daniel certainly travelled by train. But the connection to Jesse James may not be that obscure. The Leadville of 1886 was only slightly more civilized than the unnamed rough-and-tumble mining camp it had been a few years earlier. It had, in fact, been visited by such legends as Frank and Jesse James, Bat Masterson, Wyatt Earp and Doc Holliday (who lived there off and on until his death in 1887). Although the area around Leadville had been mined shortly after the '59 Rush with minimal success, it was only after the discovery of some major silver mines in the 1870s that Leadville gained national attention. The two-mile high "City of Clouds" that greeted Maggie was an exciting, romantic place to be, teeming with young, ambitious transplants.

Maggie and Daniel stayed at the Landrigans' five-room home at 529 East 5th Street. Jack worked as a blacksmith, while Mary Ann began raising the first of their 11 children. Daniel soon found work as a miner (the going rate was $3 a day). And Maggie found a job with the Daniels, Fisher & Smith dry goods store on Harrison Avenue. Her job was to sew the carpets, draperies and shades.

"She was a very capable and pleasant employee, and her work was very satisfactory to her employers, and all her fellow employees were very fond of her," fellow worker Thomas F. Cahill wrote to Maggie's son Larry years later. "She was exceptionally bright, a most interesting conversationalist, had a charming personality and this coupled with her beauty made her a very attractive woman. It is easy to understand that at about this time the handsome young Jim Brown fell in love with her."

Although Maggie would later be portrayed on stage and screen by Tammy Grimes and Debbie Reynolds, photographs show a considerably less glamorous woman — despite Tom Cahill's rather smitten description of her beauty. The red-haired, blue-eyed Maggie was also, as the Victorians would say, "buxom". The only small things about her were her hands and

This photo, one of two inscribed "To My Friend J.J. Brown In Remembrance Of Pioneer Days In Leadville, Colo. From Theodore Marx," was always kept by J.J. as a keepsake of his beloved mining town. *Photo courtesy Colorado Historical Society.*

feet which she reportedly always showed to advantage. She was attractive (and vain), but no beauty.

Maggie's young cousin Lorraine Schuck remembers it was Maggie's presence, and not her physical characteristics, that made her remarkable. "She always stood very upright, and there was something very regal about her," Lorraine recalls. Maggie was also, by all accounts, high-spirited, hot-tempered and strong-willed.

James Joseph Brown was, like Maggie, Irish Catholic. He was born September 27, 1854, in Wymert, Pennsylvania. His father, James Brown, was an Irish immigrant. His mother, the former Cecelia Palmer, was a school teacher, who encouraged her son to work his way through primary and high school in Pittston, Pennsylvania, where the family moved shortly after he was born.

J.J., as he was usually called, was bitten by the mining bug early on, but the coal fields of his home state did not hold his interest for long. It was shinier and more lucrative metals he sought, and in 1877 J.J. joined the gold rush to the Black Hills of the Dakotas. By 1880, he was in Colorado, stopping for a while in Leadville and then moving on to try his luck in the mining towns of Georgetown, Gunnison, Aspen and Ashcroft. By 1885, he had returned and settled in Leadville.

Maggie would later say she wanted to marry a rich man, so she could give to the Tobin family the comforts they never had. J.J. Brown was not rich but he was, like Maggie, ambitious and smart. His first job in Leadville in 1885 was as a miner, but he rose quickly through the ranks to shift-boss and timberman. He was foreman of the Louisville Mine by the time he and Maggie met a year later. By 1887 he was superintendent of the Louisville Mine, and in 1888 he was superintendent of the Henriette & Maid Consolidated Mining Company, at the time one of the most productive mines in the area.

"James J. Brown...[was] of that new breed of mining men who took the reins of the Cloud City's metals industry in the late eighties and early nineties," Leadville historian Edward Blair wrote. "The hit and miss devil-take-the-hindmost methods were gone, and educated, hard-driving professionals took over." Although only a few years earlier Leadville was a "poor man's camp," where anyone with a pick and shovel could start digging, those easy surface mines were soon cleaned out. It took experience to dig the deeper shafts now required, and J.J. had a reputation for being one of the camp's most knowledgeable mining engineers. (The tall, handsome, blue-eyed miner also had a reputation of another kind. One old-time Leadville resident remembers that J.J.'s female contemporaries always got "a sparkle in their eyes" when his name came up in conversation).

The courtship was quick. On September 1, 1886, Maggie and J.J. were married. J.J. was 31 years old. Maggie, who had only that year arrived in Leadville, was barely 19. The marriage was performed in Annunciation Church by Leadville's pioneer Catholic priest, Father Henry Robinson. The best man, Thomas Greeley, was a barber; the bridesmaid, Margaret Boylan, a housemaid. Among the gifts received by the couple was, appropriately, a solid silver tea service presented by the miners of the Louisville Mine. Following a trout dinner at Evergreen Lakes, Maggie and J.J. spent their honeymoon at Twin Lakes, one of the most popular summer resorts in the area.

The newlyweds lived briefly at 322 West 7th Street but soon moved up to Iron Hill, where J.J. was working. Leadville miners and their families often lived near the mines, particularly in the winter months when the journey to town, although only a few miles away, could be cold and treacherous. Their home was typical of those in outlying mountain communities — a small, two-room log cabin.

On August 30, 1887, the Browns' first child, Lawrence Palmer, was born, and in 1888 the family moved back to Leadville. Their address that year was 320 E. 9th Street. In 1889, shortly before the birth of their second and last child, Catherine Ellen — who was always known as Helen — they moved into what would be their permanent Leadville home at 300 East 7th Street.

(Years later, J.J. showed his daughter the house where she was born. "She treated it with scorn," J.J. wrote to his son Larry. "She seemed a want [sic] to forget." As an adult, Helen, like Maggie, acquired a taste for high living and Eastern society, both of which J.J. abhorred. But J.J. reminded his daughter that

Early family portrait taken in Leadville shows, left to right, Helen, J.J., Maggie, and Larry. These were, Maggie would say later, the happiest years of her life. *Photo courtesy Colorado Historical Society.*

although she had married "well," she had not married "wealth." "I told her," he wrote, "in an amusing sort of way, that it was far better than anything she could produce, better than no home a tall [sic].")

When Larry was born, Maggie went back to Hannibal for the birth. By the time Helen arrived, however, there was no need to go to Missouri since most of the Tobin family had joined the Browns in Leadville.

Maggie's half-sister Katie had, by this time, married John Becker, a Hannibal cigar-maker and confectioner. But the rest of the Tobins — John, Johanna, 21-year old William and 19-year old Ellen — sold their Missouri home and moved to Leadville. Taking a home at 708 N. Hemlock, John found work as a watchman at the Henriette & Maid Mining Company, where J.J. was a superintendent. Brother William found work as a cigar-maker, a trade he no doubt learned from his brother-in-law.

Surrounded by her successful husband, young babies, and family, these were, Maggie would later say, the happiest years of her life.

The Big Strike

They were also happy years for J.J. Mining was, he always believed, the best occupation in the world. And J.J. Brown — his business associates always referred to him by that full moniker — was esteemed as one of Leadville's finest mining men. Although never one of Leadville's elite families, the Browns did enjoy a nice home with fine furnishings.

In 1891, a group of Leadville mining men — A.V. Hunter, August R. Meyer, Max Boehmer, William Byrd Page, and John F. Campion — bought and consolidated a group of mines and leases under the name Ibex Mining Company. By 1892, J.J. acquired enough stock in Ibex to sit on the board of directors.

How could J.J. afford such a stock purchase? Maggie's sister Helen claimed it was from the sale of the Tobins' Missouri home and their life savings (despite the fact the Tobins were never wealthy). Others would say that J.J. traded

The Little Jonny Mine outside of Leadville. *Photo courtesy Colorado Historical Society.*

his know-how for a share of the Ibex venture, a common practice in those early mining days. However the money was gotten, the fact is that the Ibex stock was not worth much in those days.

In 1892, even Leadville's largest mines were suffering. The price of silver had been falling for several years, a result of overproduction and the closing of traditional silver markets. In an attempt to bolster the prices, the federal government in 1890 passed the Sherman Silver Purchase Act, which authorized the government to use silver as partial backing for paper money. But with the election of President Cleveland in 1893, the Sherman Silver Purchase Act was repealed. Leadville and the West plummeted into a depression. Silver, already at a low price of 82 cents an ounce, dropped to 61 cents. By midsummer of 1893, fully 90% of Leadville's work force was idle.

But as the price of silver fell, the price of gold — which was now the only metal backing the U.S. currency — rose. And it was gold that was destined to make the Ibex Mining Company a legend.

In 1893, despite the bad economic conditions, Ibex decided to go after a second ore contact in the Little Jonny Mine, once one of the area's major producers of silver and lead. The venture was difficult. The mine shaft hit a layer of dolomite sand and continually caved in. While the other Ibex owners were ready to abandon the operation, J.J. devised a method of using baled hay and timbers to stop the cave-ins. His persistence paid off. When the Little Jonny was opened, vast quantities of high-grade copper and gold were found. The grade of gold was so pure and the vein so wide, it was heralded as the world's richest gold strike. The Ibex Company, and its owners, were suddenly very, very rich.

And Maggie's dreams of marrying a rich man had come true.

Climbing the Social Ladder

In 1894, Maggie and J.J. followed the lead of other wealthy Leadvillites and moved to Denver. Rather than transport everything, and certainly because she was dreaming of finer things, Maggie gave all her furniture — including the brass bed which would later loom so large in the Broadway musical — to Leadville relatives. After living for a short while at 1152 York, the Browns purchased their own home at 1340 Pennsylvania Avenue. The elegant $30,000 home, which Maggie fashionably furnished in an eclectic array of styles, was located in Denver's chic Capitol Hill neighborhood.

At this point in her life, 27-year-old Maggie decided she was no longer satisfied with being just a wife and mother. She now wanted to be a woman of society, a *real* lady. And she approached that task as she did everything in life — with gusto.

"Perhaps no woman in society has ever spent more time or money becoming 'civilized' than has Mrs. Brown," the *Denver Times* reported a few years later. Indeed, within a few years of their arrival in Denver, the Browns were seasoned world-travelers, the children were enrolled in fashionable boarding schools, and Maggie was a regular item in Denver's society pages — a place she liked to see herself.

The Browns' young cousin, Lorraine, visited the Brown family home, site of all this strategic social planning. "I was impressed by three things," she reported. First, there were the coyote heads mounted in the front hall, a rather touching reminder of Maggie's and J.J.'s log cabin days when the howling of coyotes was a nightly occurrence. Second, there was the polar bear rug in the parlor. And, finally, there was the sight of Aunt Margaret's closet stacked high with shoes. "I had never seen so many shoes in my life," Lorraine recalled. Maggie's love of clothing, particularly Parisian-made, was soon to become legendary. Where nature had failed her, Maggie determined, well-paid dressmakers would succeed.

"The Brown box at the opera was the focus of many opera glasses every night," the society editors reported in 1900. And the eyes were upon Maggie who had quickly learned — in a twist of the old adage — that clothes make the woman. At the least, the clothes guaranteed good press coverage.

22

Maggie's front parlor, used for formal occasions, was furnished in a fabulous array of styles. *Photo courtesy Colorado Historical Society.*

The newspapers ran large photographs of Mrs. Brown's opera garb, "that famous gilt lace gown of hers that was described in the Parisian press as one of the most elaborate gowns ever created...Three months were consumed in the weaving of the lace, and then, after the lace was made it was spangled and embroidered in gold." To complete the ensemble, Maggie wore a lace cloak lined with ermine.

At another ball, it was Maggie's hand-painted dress which stole the show. At yet another, the "brilliantly attractive" Mrs. Brown wore a Venetian satin gown, decorated with embroidered chrysanthemums, gilded thistles, gold embroidered lace and black velvet ribbons."

Even her hairstyles garnered attention. Maggie often wore her hair piled high on her head, finished with "a gilt snake coiled about an airgrette in which glittered two large solitaires and a cluster of opals and diamonds."

(Maggie's love of jewelry is well-documented. In 1903, shortly after the Browns returned from one of their many European trips, their home was robbed. While the thief was foiled in his attempt by the screaming of the maid, the newspapers reported the house contained over $40,000 worth of jewelry, including a diamond pendant valued at $15,000.)

Maggie's social events soon became as famous as her wardrobe. And her parties, whether in the Browns' Pennsylvania Avenue home or at their country lodge, Avoca, were well-attended — despite Hollywood's claims to the contrary. At one garden party in 1910, over 800 people were expected to attend. The *al fresco* function was held on the lawn, where electric lights were strung on the trees, rare Persian rugs laid on the grass, and guests could take their refreshments in tents specially set up for the occasion. Dancing was on the third floor, with music provided by three separate bands. At this, as at her other parties, Maggie positioned musicians on the second floor balcony of her home to impress not only her guests but the whole envious neighborhood.

The papers often reported that members of European nobility were guests at the Browns' home. Three names

Maggie's passion for clothing was as great as her love of being photographed. The photo above, inscribed "With Love to Mother," shows the young Mrs. Brown in one of her first ball gowns. *Photo courtesy Colorado Historical Society.*

Photo courtesy Colorado Historical Society

Photo courtesy Colorado Historical Society

which appeared regularly were Countess Anne Leary, Baroness Von Rietzenstein — who was at the garden party — and Princess Stephanie Dolgorouki. The Countess was, in fact, a family friend who received her "title" from the Vatican. The Baroness was Maggie's sister Helen, who after a short first marriage was — at least according to Maggie — married to a German baron. (At the end of her life, Helen was married to a West Coast businessman and her letters from that time depict a deeply religious, humble woman who claimed a life-long aversion to high society.) The Princess Dolgorouki was legitimately royal. The sister-in-law of the czar, she was an exiled Russian princess who became a close friend of Maggie.

(Not all of Maggie's European friends were fancifully created. She *did* spend a great deal of time in Europe, and one newspaper account from the 1920s described her as the "uncrowned queen of smart Parisian society," an honor that, the reporter noted, she owed as much to her wit as her wealth. Among her closest friends was England's Sir Thomas Lipton, and she knew and corresponded with Edward, Duke of Windsor. "Without boasting," she once told a reporter, "I can say that I know everyone worth knowing from Moscow to the Bosphorus.")

But, despite the extravagant clothing and elaborate parties, Maggie's desire for social acceptability was serious. "It has always been to [Maggie's] credit that she has realized that social leadership required something more than the ability to pay a good chef and the taste to select a clever dressmaker," the society pages noted. Shortly after becoming wealthy, Maggie spent a winter at New York's Carnegie Institute studying languages, literature and dramatics. (Later, she travelled to Paris to have her enunciation of French perfected by a famous tutor. "I'll never forget the first time I went to him," she recalled. "He pulled a cork from a champagne bottle and ordered me to put it in my mouth — the cork, not the bottle. 'That will make you hold your mouth open when you talk,' he informed me and he didn't even smile when I told him I thought most people preferred me with it shut.")

The only known photo of Maggie in her house shows a young hostess in preparation for a dinner party. *Photo courtesy Colorado Historical Society.*

The newspapers called Maggie "self-made on a gorgeous scale." Of herself, she said, "I'm a glutton for knowledge." *Photo courtesy Colorado Historical Society.*

Charitable causes were also used as a social stepping stone. In Maggie's case, they were also an extension of her natural generosity. Catholic charities, in particular, became a lifelong interest. Both she and J.J. gave generously to Leadville's St. Vincent's Orphanage, and in Denver she raised money for St. Joseph Hospital and the Cathedral of the Immaculate Conception. In 1900, she was appointed to the prestigious position of general manager of the Catholic Fair. She also worked with Judge Ben B. Lindsey of Denver's Juvenile Court, and became a sponsor of the western branch of the Alliance Francais.

The social planning paid off. Beginning in 1894, the Browns were regularly listed in the city's social directory. That same year, Maggie became a charter member of the Denver Women's Club. Later, she became an associate member of the Denver Woman's Press Club. J.J., meanwhile, hobknobbed at the Denver Athletic Club, where he maintained a membership until his death in 1922.

Still, Maggie was not an unqualified success in Denver. The town's old guard — epitomized by Mrs. Crawford Hill — eyed her as an upstart (and, perhaps, too honest a reminder of their own past). She was never invited into the elite "Sacred 36" of the city's social directory and, in many circles, was considered coarse. Maggie was also Irish and Catholic, two social handicaps at the turn-of-the-century. But these setbacks, while frustrating, were not major. And Maggie, during these years, basked in the fame and lifestyle that money could bring.

Polly Pry Tells All

J.J., meanwhile, was increasingly uncomfortable with their new life. Except in matters pertaining to his work, he avoided the limelight that his wife now so passionately sought. During Maggie's parties he often retired, alone, to his bedroom or the furnace room to smoke cigars and drink.

The Browns also disagreed on how the children were to be raised. Maggie wanted to send the children abroad for their education; J.J. wanted them closer to home. "They went to

Paris without my consent," he wrote to Maggie Leary, his wife's old school teacher and lifetime friend, "as I had to allow Mrs. Brown to do as she pleased in this as well as other matters." To another friend he complained "She has ruined [the children] for any earthly use." Maggie was, in fact, bouncing Larry and Helen between boarding schools, often taking them out altogether to join her on her travels.

J.J. was also frustrated by his inability to work because of rheumatism and heart problems. In 1899, he suffered a stroke that, for a time at least, left him partially paralyzed. He went back to his beloved Leadville as often as his health would allow, but by the turn-of-the-century, J.J. Brown's active mining days were over.

In 1902, the Browns made what was probably their last family trip together — a world tour that included a stop in Japan. When they returned a year later, their private troubles became embarrassingly public.

In 1903, a sensational gossip magazine, *Polly Pry, A Journal of Comment and Criticism*, devoted more than a half-page of its introductory issue to what apparently was becoming quite a topic in Denver society — the adventures of Mrs. J.J. Brown.

"When is society not society," Pry began and then attacked Maggie for her lack of breeding and culture, her social ambitions, and even her physical appearance. Maggie had, Pry noted, a "face full of irregular features." Pry also reported that a few years earlier in 1897, the National Federation of Women's Clubs had convened in Denver and Mrs. Brown, in a desire to establish herself socially, had invited the most elite group members to a luncheon at Avoca. "It is boldly told that after the first course the refreshment gave out and the remaining courses were forgotten by the guests in their eagerness to watch the hostess [Maggie] emerge from a spell of hysterics, which, although a trifle distorting, cost nothing." Maggie felt the committee was at fault for not telling her how many people were coming to lunch. "Since then," the snippy Miss Pry tattled, "Mrs. Brown has not been active in club work."

Another event Maggie planned at Avoca was a stage play.

In addition to their Pennsylvania Avenue home, the Browns owned Avoca, a 240-acre ranch south of Denver which they purchased in 1895. "Milk, butter, buttermilk, smeerkase [*sic*], ice, chickens, fruit and all sorts of good things, find their way each morning, as regularly as the sun rises, from the ranch to the town residence of the Browns," reported the *Rocky Mountain News* in 1897. The bountiful ranch — extensively landscaped with orchards, grain fields and a fish lake — was the site of many of Maggie's most famous social events. Guests often traveled to the remote location by train, where a coachman would meet them at the station. *Photo courtesy Denver Public Library, Western History Department*

Avoca was also involved in one of J.J.'s most creative business ventures. The 1904 *Rocky Mountain News* reported that J.J. planned to turn his country home into the world's largest "scientific chickenry," capable of producing at least 10,000 chickens a month.

J.J.'s plan for the venture rested on William Newton, "one of the most successful chicken raisers in the southwest" who had devised a method to raise chickens "according to the latest curves and mandates laid down by science." Plans included special diets, a chicken hospital and special precautions to protect the flock against theft and predators.

Newton had come to Denver by way of Kansas where he had been involved in a similar enterprise. However, just at the time that experiment was about to reach its zenith, "one of the cyclones that has made Kansas famous came along and blew away and destroyed several thousand chickens."

Although Newton hoped to do better in Denver's less turbulent climate, the Avoca venture was an apparent failure and was never mentioned again in the papers. The Browns sold the ranch in 1906.

Avoca Lodge still stands at the corner of south Wadsworth Boulevard and west Yale Avenue. The large two-and-one-half story brick farmhouse was built in 1897. *Photo by Roger Whitacre.*

A director had been hired, advertising sent out and all was going well until the star, Jane Oakes, declared her cost for appearing would be at least $1,000. The event was cancelled, Pry reported, and "the originator of the idea is recuperating from a severe social strain at the mountain resorts."

And, while she was on the subject of Avoca, Polly questioned the origin of the lodge's name, calling it pretentious.

A more diplomatic person, and Maggie was not the only social butterfly attacked by Polly Pry, might have ignored the article. But Maggie fired off a letter printed in the next issue of *Polly Pry*. Written in an affected, stilted style which was as unnatural to Maggie as the social territory on which she was now treading, the letter explained her reasons for naming her lodge "Avoca" (after a poem by Thomas Moore). Polly, never missing an opportunity to ridicule, printed Maggie's letter verbatim, complete with all its misspellings, awkward phrases and grammatical errors.

"Enclosed find the poem which I have committed the sacrilege by desecrating its title 'Avoca' in applying it to a homestead in a valley of Colorado," Maggie wrote. "May I be pardoned of so grave a crime? If after leaving the Smelter smoke of Denver, travesing miles of uninteresting stretch of country, in reaching the sumit 'behold' 'the hand made of Lord,' and the sublime work of nature a panoramic view of a most picturesque valley bursts upon men."

The letter continued along that vein for two more paragraphs and was signed,
"Truley Yours,
Margaret Tobin Brown."

But if Polly Pry's criticism stung, they were nothing compared to what followed. In 1904, the newspapers reported that J.J. was being sued for alienation of affection by Harry D. Call. Call charged, and the details appeared in the daily newspapers, that 48-year-old J.J. had seduced Call's 22-year-old wife Maude. It was while J.J. was "taking the waters" at a spa in Pueblo — presumably for his rheumatism — that he met Maude, "a small blonde with a splendid figure and a rather demure face, lighted only by the eyes that laugh." Call

The Brown children on an outing with their pony. The woman on the porch appears to be Maggie. *Photo courtesy Colorado Historical Society.*

John and Johanna Tobin lived in the Brown family home until their deaths, respectively, in 1899 and 1905. This photo shows the Tobins in the back parlor, later converted into a library. *Photo courtesy Colorado Historical Society.*

Helen Brown, seen here as a young girl, grew to be an attractive woman, frequently mentioned in Denver's society pages. *Photo courtesy Denver Public Library, Western History Department.*

Like Helen, Larry was educated in Europe. This photo was taken in Paris. *Photo courtesy Colorado Historical Society.*

sued J.J. for $50,000, plus legal costs. No record of the outcome has been found. Polly Pry wrote a poem about the incident.

These years were difficult for Maggie, J.J. and their teenage children. Daughter Helen, who was quite beautiful and easily gained the social attention her mother sought, remembered these years as sad and unhappy ones. "The terrible situation which existed between mother and father was the tragedy of my childhood," she later wrote.

Indeed, J.J. and Maggie spent very little time together during the next few years. Mining speculation and real estate deals took J.J. to Cuba, Arizona, Utah and California, where he found the warmer climate more comfortable. Maggie traveled extensively in Europe, where she found the social situation more stimulating and, perhaps, more accepting. She also spent a great deal of time in the posh Eastern resort town of Newport, Rhode Island, where the Browns had rented a cottage. Finally in 1909, after nearly 23 years of marriage, the couple separated.

Maggie would later say it was J.J. who demanded the separation, despite her fantastic claim that on two occasions he had tried to shoot her and she survived only by wrestling the gun away from him. She also claimed — in a version that was probably closer to the truth — that he simply asked her to leave him alone. Daughter Helen believed it was Maggie's love of fame and high society that drove them apart. Helen later wrote of her mother: "She was not entirely to blame in the trouble with father, not originally, because he was difficult, hot tempered in the extreme and hard to please...But whereas he tried and did mend his ways and controlled himself more and more as he grew older...she succumbed more and more to what became...a ruling passion in her life."

According to the arrangements of the legal separation, Maggie received a $540 cash settlement and maintained possession of their Pennsylvania Avenue home. In addition, she received $700 a month from J.J. which, combined with stock dividends, enabled her to continue her travels in America and Europe.

The Titanic

In 1912, Maggie was touring Europe when she received word that her grandson was ill. Lawrence Palmer Jr., always known as "Pat," was Larry's infant son, a result of his 1910 marriage to Eileen Horton. Maggie immediately made arrangements to return to the states, and booked passage on the *RMS Titanic*.

In an era when transatlantic luxury liners were the last word in travel, the *Titanic* was a wonder. Built by the British White Star Lines at a cost of $10 million, the ship weighed over 46,000 tons and was 882.5 feet in length. But her size, though impressive, did not compare with her luxurious appointments. "There will never be another like her," said Baker Charles Burgess in Walter Lord's *A Night to Remember.* "They can make them bigger and faster, but it was the care and effort that went into her. She was a beautiful, wonderful ship."

The features of this "floating palace" included a glass-domed staircase that served seven of her eleven decks, a lounge outfitted in imitation of the Palace of Versailles, a gymnasium with the latest electrical exercise equipment from Wiesbaden, a reception room for private parties, a library, a saltwater swimming pool, a squash racquet court, a hospital room with modern operating equipment, a photographic darkroom and a Turkish bath that boasted a "completeness of equipment not surpassed by any baths ashore." The first-class rooms, the most luxurious of which cost $4,350 for the six-day maiden voyage, had free-standing beds rather than berths, made possible by the steadiness of the ship.

The ship's builders also boasted that the ship was "practically unsinkable," which the popular press quickly translated into "unsinkable." Indeed, much was made of the *Titanic's* claim to be a "dependable Atlantic Ocean ferry," which would meet tight schedules despite bad weather conditions — and in complete safety. The ship's hull was double-bottomed, as thick as 6 feet 3 inches at some points. Moreover, the hull was divided into 16 watertight compartments which were to keep the ship afloat in case of disaster. It was only after the tragedy that the ship's builders were to learn of the inadequacy of their design.

Besides Maggie, the *Titanic's* first-class passenger list included an impressive number of American and European celebrities: J.J. Astor, great-grandson of the John Jacob Astor who had made a fortune in the fur trade; millionaire Benjamin Guggenheim; Charles Hays, president of the Grand Trunk Railway; journalist Jacques Futrelle; Isador Straus, a partner in the R.H. Macy & Company; English evangelist and writer W.T. Stead; and J. Bruce Ismay, owner of the White Star Line. Of the above, only Maggie and Ismay would survive.

Also aboard were hundreds of third-class passengers, the majority of whom were European immigrants on their way to reap the rewards of the great American dream — of which Maggie's life was such an outstanding example.

It was cold and gray when Maggie and the other passengers boarded the *Titanic* on the evening of April 10, 1912. In an article she later wrote for the *Newport Herald*, Maggie reported she had some warning of the disaster: "The writer [referring to herself] sought some exceedingly intellectual and much traveled acquaintances, a Mrs. Bucknell, whose husband had founded the Bucknell University of Philadelphia and Dr. Brewe of Philadelphia, who has done much in scientific research. During our conversation that I had with [Mrs. Bucknell] on the tender while waiting for the *Titanic*, she said she feared boarding the ship, she had evil forebodings that something might happen...We laughed at her premonitions, and shortly afterwards sought our quarters."

On the evening of April 14, the fifth day of the journey, Mrs. Bucknell's premonitions proved true.

Maggie described the events of that evening: "Anxious to finish a book, I stretched on the brass bed, at the side of which was a lamp. So completely absorbed in my reading, I gave little thought to the crash that struck at my window overhead and threw me to the floor. Picking myself up I proceeded to see what the steamer had struck. On emerging from the stateroom, I found many men in the gangway in

Surpassing the Greatest Buildings and Memorials of Earth

The Largest and Finest Steamers in the World ☆ "OLYMPIC" AND "TITANIC" ☆ White Star Line's New Leviathans   882½ Feet Long   92½ Feet Broad   45,000 Tons

1 Bunker Hill Monument, Boston — 221 Feet High
2 Public Buildings, Philadelphia — 534 Feet High
3 Washington Monument, Washington — 555 Feet High
4 Metropolitan Tower, New York — 700 Feet High
5 New Woolworth Building, New York — 750 Feet High

6 White Star Line's Triple Screw Steamers "OLYMPIC" and "TITANIC" — 882½ Feet Long
7 Cologne Cathedral, Cologne, Germany — 516 Feet High
8 Grand Pyramid, Gizeh, Africa — 451 Feet High
9 St. Peter's Church, Rome, Italy — 448 Feet High

41

The first-class staterooms on the *Titanic* had free-standing beds rather than berths, made possible by the steadiness of the ship.

The ship's gymnasium featured the most modern exercise equipment available.

their pajamas... All seemed to be quietly listening, thinking nothing serious had occurred, though realizing at the time that the engines had stopped immediately after the crash and the boat was at a standstill."

That evening, the ship's captain and crew had received numerous warnings of ice in the area. And, since the night was calm, there were no breaking waves to help the sailors locate icebergs. Still, for reasons that would be hotly debated for years, the *Titanic* charged ahead at its nearly top speed of 25 knots. By the time the lookout saw the iceberg, it was too late to successfully change course. Shortly before midnight, the *Titanic* struck ice.

The deck crew did not immediately realize the extent of the damage. Some thought the ship had only been grazed by the iceberg. Although Maggie claims to have been thrown from her bed, other passengers felt only a slight jar. Many passengers, like Maggie, suspected something was wrong only because the engines had shut down.

But the men in the boiler room immediately realized the extent of damage, as they literally leapt for their lives to avoid the rushing water caused by the 300-foot gash in the ship's hull.

After the crash, Maggie returned to her stateroom. But increasing confusion in the hall caused her to investigate further. "I again looked out," she wrote, "and I saw a man whose face was blanched, his eyes protruding, wearing the look of a haunted creature. He was grasping for breath, and in an undertone he gasped, 'Get your life-saver.'" By 12:15 a.m., the ship was sending its first distress signal — and preparing the lifeboats.

Maggie found the other members of her party on deck. "Mrs. Bucknell approached me and whispered 'Didn't I tell you something was going to happen?'" Maggie recalled. After seeing Mrs. Bucknell safely loaded into a lifeboat, Maggie went "to see what was being done with the boats on the other side."

Maggie later claimed she never feared for her personal safety. "If the worst should happen," she confidently declared, "I could swim out." But she was never able to prove her swimming ability. "Suddenly I saw a shadow," she wrote, "and a few second later, I was taken hold of, and with the words 'You are going too,' was dropped fully four feet in the lowering lifeboat."

On looking around, Maggie discovered there were about 14 women in the boat and one man. In fact, it was one's sex that was the greatest determinant of who would live or die that night. The ship was woefully unequipped, carrying only enough lifeboats for 1,000 people despite the 2,300 passengers and crew members on board. (As a result of the *Titanic* disaster, there would be major changes in maritime law concerning lifeboat requirements and procedures.) It was "women and children first," and most of those lost at sea were men.

The one male occupant of Maggie's lifeboat was the ship's quartermaster. "He was shivering like an aspen," Maggie remarked. He "burst out in a frightened voice, and warned us of the fate that awaited us, telling us our task in rowing away from the sinking ship was futile, as she was so large that in sinking she would take everything for miles around down with her suction, and if we escaped that the boilers would burst and rip up the bottom of the sea, tearing the icebergs asunder and completely submerge us."

But Maggie ignored the shivering sailor, grabbed hold of the oars, and ordered another young woman to do the same. "As we pulled away from the boat, we heard sounds of firing, and were told later that it was officers shooting as they were letting down the boats from the steamer, trying to prevent those from the lower decks jumping into the lifeboats. Others said [correctly] it was the boilers."

At 2:30 a.m., April 15, the *Titanic* sank. "Suddenly [there was] a rift in the water, the sea opened up and the surface foamed like giant arms spread around the ship, and the vessel disappeared from sight, and not a sound was heard," Maggie wrote. Of the approximately 2,300 aboard, 1,600 were lost.

Maggie's lifeboat pulled away from the scene. "Our quar-

The "Unsinkable Mrs. Brown" presented Captain A.H. Rostrom and the crew of the *Carpathia* with a loving cup for their rescue of the *Titanic* survivors. *Photo courtesy Colorado Historical Society.*

termaster...with an attitude like someone preaching to the multitude, fanning the air with his hands, recommenced his tirade of evil forebodings, telling us we were likely to drift for days...He most forcibly impressed upon us that there was no water in the casks in the lifeboats and no bread, no compass and no chart." The only thing that distracted the sailor from his miserable chant was the sight of a flask of brandy produced by one of the women. Despite his pleas, she refused to give it to him.

At approximately 4:30 a.m., Maggie saw a flash of light — "a falling star," declared the pessimistic quartermaster. But the light was the approaching *Carpathia* which, though not the nearest ship to the *Titanic*, was the first to answer its distress call.

Once on board the *Carpathia*, Maggie helped organize rescue efforts. Her knowledge of foreign languages enabled her to successfully aid the immigrant passengers. She made lists of survivors and arranged for that information to be radioed ahead to their families. And, together with a committee of other wealthy survivors, Maggie helped raise money for destitute victims. Before the *Carpathia* reached New York, nearly $10,000 was pledged.

When the *Carpathia* docked in New York, Maggie was surrounded by reporters and was asked to what she attributed her survival. "Typical Brown luck," she reportedly replied, "We're unsinkable."

In Denver, J.J. Brown was heard to comment, "She's too mean to sink."

The Unsinkable Mrs. Brown

The *Titanic* tragedy made Maggie a national celebrity. It was a role she was born to play.

By the time she arrived in Denver, the media was clamoring to interview the "Unsinkable Mrs. Brown." From her suite in the Brown Palace Hotel (her Pennsylvania Avenue home had been rented), she told and retold her version of the *Titanic* adventure, also adding stories of how she had survived a cyclone on the Mississippi and a typhoon on

The *Titanic* tragedy turned Maggie into a national celebrity. *Photo courtesy Colorado Historical Society.*

the Indian Ocean. Newspapers lavished whole pages on her heroics.

Even Denver society capitulated. Among those welcoming her back was Mrs. Crawford Hill, who hosted a luncheon in her honor. Although not the beginning of a long friendship, it must have pleased Maggie to have conquered that last bastion of Denver society. Even Polly Pry did not matter now.

The *Titanic* also turned Maggie into a political figure. She asked the Denver Women's Club to petition Congress for maritime reform. The unwritten law of the sea, which declared women and children first, was tragically immoral said Maggie, pointing to the hundreds of destitute widows and children left behind by the sea tragedy. "Their husbands went down to practically painless deaths, while they are left to suffer living deaths," she said.

In 1914, she ran, unsuccessfully, for the U.S. Senate. (She was not the first Brown with political ambitions. In 1908, J.J. ran, also unsuccessfully, for Denver City Alderman.) With the outbreak of World War I, Maggie volunteered, through the press, to serve as an army nurse and offered her Newport cottage as a naval hospital. When both requests were turned down, she announced she would serve her country as an entertainer for the armed forces. She specialized in roles made famous by Sarah Bernhardt for which, headlines on both sides of the Atlantic would report, she was named to the French Legion of Honor. She also became a member of the National Women's Party and met with President Calvin Coolidge to seek his endorsement for the Equal Rights Amendment.

It was during these years that the legends began to take root. Numerous magazines and papers popularized Maggie's life, creating "facts" where the truth would not do. Nearly every activity of the "Unsinkable Mrs. Brown" — whether it was her work on behalf of suffragette causes or her penchant for yodeling at parties — was tracked in the press.

And, once again, she was controversial. After the *Titanic* tragedy, she developed what would become the lifelong

This frame house on the corner of Bellevue Avenue and Redwood Street in Newport, Rhode Island, was rented by Maggie from 1913 to 1922 as a summer residence. Here, she created as much of a social sensation as she did in Denver. For one party, she startled Newport society by turning her home into an "Indian Grotto" with *papier-mâché* stalagtites, Navajo rugs, artificial flowers and a sunken fishbowl in the center of the dining table. *Photo courtesy Molly Brown House Museum.*

habit of making her opinions, no matter how inflammatory (or unfounded), public. *Titanic* owner Bruce Ismay caused the tragedy, Maggie declared, because he insisted the ship go at full speed so he could be on time for a New York dinner party. She also said the *Titanic* crew was a "slew of scrubs" who were determined that "American nabobs" not survive. While these sensational comments did not result in lawsuits, others did. A 1913 lawsuit by a dentist made front page news. In 1920, Mrs. Celine Villemin, who organized the Universiti Francais for war relief work, sued Maggie for $100,000 because Maggie said the organization had been formed for commercial purposes. That same year another New York woman, Mrs. Maria F. Wathey, sued Maggie for $25,000 for slander. Regarding the latter lawsuit, Maggie said Mrs. Wathey had annoyed her "by running up and down her stairway while attired only in a nightgown."

"Publicity is the very breath of this woman's nostrils," hissed Colorado Senator Helen R. Robinson in 1920, regarding yet another slanderous statement made by Maggie, this time about the senator's handling of charitable contributions. Many were inclined to agree with Mrs. Robinson's assessment.

Family Troubles

During this period, J.J. was having his own troubles. In 1919, Mrs. Sabra Simpson sued J.J. for breach of promise. The "buxom widow" claimed she had lived with J.J. in California and Colorado and he had promised to marry her so that she "might share in his millions." J.J. claimed he had only a passing acquaintance with Mrs. Simpson, a one-time actress.

Even if Mrs. Simpson had succeeded in marrying J.J., she wouldn't have shared in his millions. By 1920, the Brown family fortune was dwindling.

From the time they became rich, both Maggie and J.J. had been exceedingly generous to their extended families, financing business ventures and paying for the education of nieces and nephews. In addition, both the Brown children — Larry and Helen — drew heavily on their father's support.

The family situation was strained in later years, but J.J., Helen, Larry and Maggie managed to stop squabbling long enough to pose for this family portrait. *Photo courtesy Colorado Historical Society.*

When J.J. retired from active mining shortly after the Little Jonny strike, he rechanneled his energies into real estate ventures and mining speculation. *Photo courtesy Colorado Historical Society.*

This coat was one of Maggie's favorites, made of mustard-colored velvet trimmed with fox fur. The ever-present swagger stick, she said, was for fallen arches. *Photo courtesy Denver Public Library, Western History Department.*

In 1915, Larry and Eileen were divorced. They remarried in 1917, reportedly through Maggie's influence, shortly before Larry went off to serve as a captain with the American Expeditionary Forces in World War I. When he returned from the war "gassed and verging on tuberculosis," the family situation did not improve. The considerable correspondence which exists between Larry and "The Chief" — as the children affectionately called their father — shows that J.J. was concerned about Larry's instability. Pick a career, the father told his son, and stick with it. Larry, meanwhile, tried a number of occupations: mining, insurance sales, construction, golf course management, even ranching. In 1927, after a considerable estrangement, Larry and Eileen were divorced for a second and final time.

But Larry's inability to take hold of his life is understandable. During these years, he spent a great deal of time and energy serving as referee in a family situation that was becoming increasingly troubled.

Although Maggie and J.J. saw virtually nothing of each other, they fought passionately. Both were convinced they were being followed by the other. (In fact, J.J. did suggest to Larry that detectives follow Maggie and prove her insane, but this apparently was never done.) Maggie claimed J.J. was spying on her because he wanted a divorce. J.J. felt Maggie, who claimed the financial arrangements of the separation agreement were inadequate, wanted to track his business dealings more closely. "Your mother," J.J. despaired to Larry, "is my greatest enemy."

Helen, in the meantime, was embarrassed by her mother's increasingly eccentric behavior and clothing, and communicated to her mainly through Larry. (When Helen married New York publisher George J. Benziger in 1913, the wedding was attended by J.J. but not Maggie, who was traveling in Europe.) Indeed, some aspects of Maggie's personal life became extremely erratic during this time. Her letters, once characterized by neat handwriting, had been reduced to an illegible scrawl. Sentences or thoughts rarely connected. Some Tobin family members contacted Larry about their

The Browns' Pennsylvania Avenue home was embellished with sphinxes and lions, earning it the name "House of Lions." "Some people smirked when I brought home ancient statuary from Egypt and decorated up a few acres of the Rocky Mountains for my home," said Maggie, "but I am sure that those who know the place will agree that culture knows no boundaries and that fine arts are international." *Photo courtesy Denver Public Library, Western History Department.*

Larry served as a captain with the American Expeditionary Forces in World War I. *Photo courtesy Colorado Historical Society.*

Larry's first wife, Eileen Horton, with their two children, Betty and Lawrence, Jr. It was Lawrence Jr.'s illness which prompted Maggie, who was traveling in Europe, to book passage on the *Titanic*. After their 1927 divorce, Larry married Mildred Gregory, an actress who appeared in a number of Hollywood films. *Photo courtesy Colorado Historical Society.*

Helen Brown Benziger with her two children, James and Peter. *Photo courtesy Colorado Historical Society.*

fears for their sister's mental and physical state, but he had no more control over his mother's activities than they.

Old Leadville

In 1920, J.J. made what would be his final trip to Leadville. After years of living in hotels, J.J. finally succumbed to his daughter's demand to live with her. On the trip from California to Helen's New York home, he stopped over in Leadville. Although his doctor warned him not to stay long in Colorado because of the altitude, "once there he was so happy to be back with his old cronies, he dallied and over two weeks passed," his daughter would later report. Indeed, a letter from J.J. to Larry describes his joy at being back in Leadville among his "own kind." This, after all, was a man's town — a working man's town — and money never brought J.J. as much satisfaction as being in the mines of Leadville.

"O, Leadville is very very quiet but I have wished a thousand times that I could withstand her winters and then here I would stay forever as long as I could live," he wrote. "It will be a great camp again, and I feel just now as though I could do more than my share in the way of redeeming the old camp, and, bring it back to its own... O, if I could only stand the cold of old Leadville."

But it was not to be. After a long lingering illness at Helen's home in Hempstead, New York, J.J. suffered a series of heart attacks and was hospitalized. He died, alone, at dawn on September 5, 1922.

Although always very concerned as to how the Brown money was divided between Maggie and the children in his lifetime, J.J. died without leaving a signed will, despite having had at least two drawn up. The result was an emotional and legal storm that would take years to settle. Finally, after a myriad of suits and countersuits between Maggie and the children, the estate was settled in 1927. Of the approximate $238,000 J.J. left behind, Maggie received $20,000 in cash and securities, and the interest on a $100,000 trust fund set up in her name. The remainder was divided equally between Helen and Larry.

During the rest of Maggie's life, her children followed her comings and goings the same way as everyone else — by reading the newspapers. Wherever she went, whatever she did, this remarkable woman from Colorado attracted national attention. In 1925, she again escaped tragedy when she survived a fire at the Breakers Hotel in Palm Beach. When the city of Hannibal, Missouri, dedicated a statue to Tom Sawyer and Huckleberry Finn in 1926, Maggie was there and told reporters she planned to publish her autobiography. Tentatively titled *The Course of Human Events*, the book never materialized. In 1927, the papers reported that she intended to adopt two children, George Seal and Peggy Shaw. (Although the adoptions never took place, son Larry considered taking legal action to prevent the adoptions — declaring Maggie could barely take care of herself let alone anyone else.) That same year, the newspapers also announced that Maggie would marry the Duke of Chatre. The next day, the Parisian papers declared the Duke's title had been extinct for years and the engagement was off.

Still, Maggie's dedication to charitable and civic causes continued. In 1927, she became involved with one of Denver's first historic preservation projects. When she learned that the home that once belonged to Eugene Field, the childhood poet who penned "Wynken, Blynken and Nod," was in danger of demolition, she purchased it, donated it to the city, and had it moved to a new location in Denver's Washington Park where it still stands today. (Almost 50 years later, the "saving" of Maggie's home would launch the founding of Historic Denver Incorporated, the city's only private preservation organization.)

And, like J.J., Maggie stayed close to Leadville, often visiting Brown family relatives. She usually stayed at the town's Vendome Hotel, where J.J. had stayed on his last visit and where they had stayed together on their joint trips to town. Weather permitting, she would also visit their old cabin on Iron Hill. She would even journey up to Evergreen and Twin Lakes where they had enjoyed their honeymoon.

But by 1930 the visits to Colorado became less frequent, as

Maggie spent most of her later years in European and East Coast resorts. *Photo courtesy Colorado Historical Society.*

Maggie spent more and more time in the East. Now her appearance in Denver was something of an oddity. No longer was she the flamboyant, outspoken young wife of J.J. Brown, she was an aging image of a world that was rapidly fading into history.

A *Denver Post* reporter recalls seeing Maggie for the first time in 1930:

"I had no idea then who she was. But her flamboyant appearance made a lasting impression...

"Her imposing stature was heightened by a pink plume billowing over the hat she wore at a dashing angle. It exposed her crimpled hair, a flashing henna shade that clashed with her flabby, rouged cheeks. A stringy feather boa fluttered over her buxom bosom.

"Her purple silk dress clung to her stiffly corseted figure and sagged around her ankles. They bagged in wrinkled stockings over the tops of her tiny button shoes. Like her wee pouchy, tassled handbag, her feet seemed too small for the rest of her.

"Yet she had great dignity. There was something terribly regal about her. Perhaps it was her tall, gold-tipped swagger stick, or the way she peered through the lorgnettes on a gold chain around her bulging neck. Perhaps it was the way she gazed over my head as she strutted pompously, though with faltering steps, down 17th Street, like a Civil War Veteran.

"Heads turned at the sight of her, and as she passed by, she left in her wake an essence of violets, rose-water and moth-balls. Everything about her was amazing and fascinating...I sensed that she was a brave and lonely woman probably living in the heyday of her past."

Helen had predicted a lonely "deserted old age" for her mother, and that dire forecast seems to have come true. Estranged from her family and children, Maggie was, by 1931, living in New York's Barbizon Hotel, a popular residence for young aspiring actresses (and an unlikely one for an elderly widow). On October 26, 1932, 65-year-old Margaret Tobin Brown suffered two strokes of "apoplexy" and died, alone, in her hotel suite. While her death made head-

"A career as colorful, dramatic and inspiring as a western sunset came to an abrupt close," said one Denver reporter about Maggie's death in 1932. "She was a definite, fearless personality. She knew what she wanted and went after it, and seldom failed of her goal." *Photo courtesy Denver Public Library, Western History Department.*

lines in the Denver papers, her remains were not returned to Colorado. After a simple funeral service Maggie was buried, next to J.J., in Long Island's Holy Rood Cemetery.

Although the newspapers reported that Maggie bequeathed large amounts of money to her family, there was, in fact, nothing left.

After a few years of living in California, Larry Brown and his second wife, the former Mildred Gregory, moved to Leadville. Here, in a move which would have pleased his father, Larry concentrated on mining activities, even serving as a director of the Ibex Mining Company. He died in Leadville in 1949.

Helen, who lived to see her mother's life dramatized on stage and screen, died in New York in 1969.

History of the Molly Brown House Museum

The Molly Brown House Museum, as it is now known, sits on land which was first platted in 1868 as part of the John W. Smith Addition to Denver. In 1887, as the area was developing into an upper middle-class residential neighborhood, the vacant building site was purchased by Isaac and Mary Large for $4,000. Later, the Larges bought an additional four feet of property for $500, making the total site 70½ by 125 feet.

Although the Larges oversaw the completion of their spacious, three-story home in 1890, they did not enjoy it for long. Mary Large's health was poor, and the family moved to the rural and more "healthful" suburban community of Montclair. On April 3, 1894, Large sold the house for $30,000 to James Joseph Brown. In 1898, title was transferred to Maggie's name, perhaps because of J.J.'s deteriorating health.

Although Maggie owned the house until her death, neither she nor her family lived there continuously during these years. In 1902, while the Browns were on a round-the-world trip, the home was rented to Governor and Mrs. James Orman of Pueblo, making it the Governor's Mansion for that year. After Maggie and J.J.'s separation in 1909, Maggie spent increasingly less time in Denver. When she did come back, she often took a suite at the Brown Palace Hotel. From

The Molly Brown House as it appears today. *Photo courtesy Molly Brown House Museum.*

Meredith Willson's stageplay, *The Unsinkable Molly Brown,* made Maggie (who was never called Molly) a national celebrity. Tammy Grimes played the title role in the Broadway production. *Photo courtesy New York Public Library at Lincoln Center.*

The MGM screen version of *The Unsinkable Molly Brown* featured Debbie Reynolds, on the left, and Harve Presnell, center, in the roles of Maggie and J.J.

1911-1919, the home was rented to the Cosgriff family who, when they left, took with them the library bookcases that they apparently bought from Maggie. In 1920, the home was rented to the Keiser family. In 1926, Maggie took legal action to evict tenant Lucille Hubbel, who was subletting rooms. At that point, Maggie herself converted her home into a boarding house under the supervision of her housekeeper, Ella Grable.

A friend of the family visited the house during this time and reported that Mrs. Grable was unable to keep the house fully rented. The rooms were not modern enough, he reported, commenting on the changing architectural tastes of America.

The neighborhood also had changed over the years, declining as Denver's "fashionable" moved farther south and east. When Maggie died in 1932, at the height of the depression, the house was appraised at $6,000, with a $3,100 mortgage against it. The household furnishings, which included two hand-carved mahogany four-poster beds, were auctioned off for $200.

In 1933, Jay Weatherly bought the house for $5,000. During the next few years title tranferred three more times. While the exterior remained virtually unchanged, the interior was modernized extensively, to the point that it bore little resemblance to the Victorian showplace it had been in Maggie's day. In 1958, the home was bought by Art Leisenring, who lived in it and operated it as a gentlemen's boarding house. Leisenring knew of Maggie — who was now being memorialized on stage and screen as *The Unsinkable Molly Brown* — and tried to get others interested in its restoration. But Victorian homes were not popular in those days, and historic preservation projects were rare. By the late 1960's, maintenance of the house had become oppressive and Leisenring leased it to the City's Juvenile Court as a home for wayward girls.

Finally in 1970, Denver resident Christine Kosewick, believing the house was in danger of demolition, wrote a letter to Colorado First Lady Ann Love. "Won't Denver

By the 1960s the Molly Brown House had fallen on hard times, serving as a men's boarding house and, later, as a home for wayward girls. *Photo courtesy Denver Public Library, Western History Department.*

recognize Molly in some way," Kosewick implored. Ann Love referred Kosewick to Bob Sheets, executive director of the Colorado Council on the Arts and Humanities. Sheets, who had also talked with Leisenring about the future of the house, turned to Ken Watson for help. Watson, a professional photographer and amateur preservationist, banded together a small group of concerned citizens who, on December 11, 1970, incorporated themselves as Historic Denver, Inc., and made a grass roots effort to save the Molly Brown House. Through a massive appeal in the media and a variety of fundraising efforts, including tours of the unrestored house, Historic Denver, Inc., successfully purchased the home for $80,000 in 1971. Over the next ten years, the group raised over $180,000 to restore the house to the way it was when Maggie lived there.

Today, Historic Denver, Inc., has grown to be one of the nation's largest and most powerful local preservation groups. Its activities have branched out to include a neighborhood revitalization project in Denver's Curtis Park, the restoration of the Grant-Humphreys Mansion, the creation of Victorian Ninth Street Park at the Auraria Higher Education Center, major publications on Denver history and architecture, the preservation of the Justina Ford home, and the restoration of Denver's major Art Deco theatre, the Paramount.

The Molly Brown House Museum, meanwhile, has become a major tourist attraction in the state. Each year approximately 40,000 people visit the house to learn about the lifestyle enjoyed by Victorian Denver's upper-middle class — and gain a glimpse into the life of Denver's unsinkable lady.

Architectural Notes

Although architect William Lang did not design the Molly Brown House for Maggie Brown, they were a good match of personalities. The house Lang designed was elegantly chic, thoroughly modern, exuberantly eclectic, and — like all of Lang's buildings — hard to define.

The Molly Brown House, on the right, was built at the same time as the Everts home on the left. Both were designed by William Lang. The Everts house, now demolished, later became the home of Joshua and Victoria Monti, two well-known Denver pioneers and good friends of Maggie's. The house featured a stone retaining wall, a feature which the Browns obviously admired and later reproduced on their home. *Photo courtesy Denver Public Library, Western History Department.*

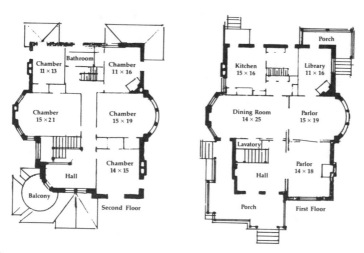

The Lang and Pugh original floor plans for the Molly Brown House. *Photo courtesy Denver Public Library, Western History Department.*

William Lang first appeared in the *Denver Directory* in 1886. By the time he left in 1893, his legacy included a number of buildings considered among Denver's finest. They are also among its most eclectic.

"He never built a building in a clear, nameable style," wrote architectural historian Richard Brettell in *Historic Denver, Its Architects and Architecture 1858-1893*. Like all eclectic architects, Lang and his lesser-known partner Marshall Pugh liked to draw from a variety of historical and architectural sources. One building could combine a Gothic tower, Romanesque arches, Eastlake ornamentation, Art Nouveau-style stained glass, and Queen Anne detailing. "It was," Brettell observed, "an architecture of the melting pot."

Although Lang and Pugh designed everything from cottages to large commercial buildings, their clients were, for the most part, Denver's burgeoning upper-middle class. As such, many Lang homes were built in the then newly-developing Capitol Hill area, located directly east of the state capitol and home to some of the city's wealthiest families. These buildings were not mansions, but rather large, well-built homes, luxuriously appointed and individually unique.

The Molly Brown House is basically Queen Anne, with its paneled gables, pinwheel plan and half-timbering. Less typical are the Romanesque arches and the stone massing. It is built of rusticated lava stone, probably quarried in the Castle Rock area, trimmed with sandstone. The wooden trim has been restored to its 1910 salmon color.

When the Browns purchased the home in 1894, they made a number of changes. The original wooden shingle roof was replaced with more "modern" and fireproof French tiles, and the two small open frame porches in the rear of the building were replaced with a large enclosed brick porch. The most drastic change, however, was to the front of the building. Originally, the front steps led directly from the sidewalk to the porch. The Browns put up a sidewalk-level retaining wall, behind which sandstone steps turned south before entering the porch. They also replaced the wooden porch bannisters with sandstone columns. Since it was Historic Denver's goal to restore the house to the way it appeared *at the time Maggie lived there*, all these changes have been maintained.

By the time Historic Denver purchased the house in 1971, the interior had been radically altered. Walls had been added, floors had been refloored with wood and covered with linoleum, and the walls replastered, painted, then repainted and papered. Curators had to resort to microscopic paint analysis, the examination of original building fragments, and the discovery of "ghost marks" or construction scars to determine what was original and what was remodeled.

But the greatest aid in restoring the house proved to be Maggie herself. In 1910, Maggie held a lavish garden party for which she hired a photographer to record the floral decorations. It is these photographs that enabled Historic Denver to authentically restore the house — right down to the placement of the seams in the bedspreads.

The 1910 photographs also show that Maggie's household furnishings were as fashionable as her wardrobe. Furnishings were a combination of Moorish, Gothic, Oriental and Eastlake styles. Many were mementoes acquired on travels. "Maggie always had the latest," reports one curator. "If the platform rocker came in, she had it. If wicker furniture came in, she had that."

The house also boasted the most modern conveniences. It was built with both indoor plumbing and electrical wiring, and was originally heated with gravity air which introduces heat into each chamber through decorative wall grates. Later, the Browns switched to hot water heat, installing the gold-painted radiators that can still be seen throughout the house and which are lavishly detailed with cupids and little fishes. Another modern convenience was the hand-crank telephone seen in the front entry hall. The Browns' exchange was A-1466.

Visitors to the house are sometimes surprised how "small" the house is as compared to the movie version. Yet the house

The front porch of the Molly Brown House Museum still features the tile floor seen in this 1910 photograph. *Photo courtesy Denver Public Library, Western History Department.*

The light fixture, anaglypta wall covering and stained glass seen in this 1910 photograph of the entranceway are still intact. The spindles on the stairway are machine-turned, which was considered more fashionable at the turn-of-the-century than hand-carved ones. *Photo courtesy Colorado Historical Society.*

Maggie had built-in bookcases installed in the library and filled them with books. Her literary tastes were wide-ranging, if not genuine. "If you speak to Mrs. Brown of the Chaucerian period of English literature she will probably tell you that she is very fond of Zola, and if you change to Zola and descant on French realism she suddenly remembers that Scott is one of her favorite authors," sniped one Newport social critic. "Thus, in a trice, you receive intimate knowledge of the tremendous scope of Mrs. Brown's excursions in literature." *Photo courtesy Denver Public Library, Western History Department.*

The kitchen area was the most difficult to restore, since it was not photographed in Maggie's day and had been extensively remodeled. When the home's original floor plans were discovered in 1976, curators were delighted to find that their restoration, based on microscopic analysis and "ghost marks," was correct. *Photo by Roger Whitacre.*

"J.J.'s Room," upholstered in green silk tapestry, is the largest bedroom in the house. The dresser covers the fireplace in this 1910 photo. *Photo courtesy Colorado Historical Society.*

"Molly's Room" is the only upstairs bedroom with a bay window. The completely restored room, as seen in this recent photo, features lace curtains and wicker furniture. *Photo by Roger Whitacre.*

is large by modern standards. Each of the three stories is 2573 sq. ft., for a total of 7719 sq. ft. The basement is an additional 1900 sq. ft.

The first floor features six main rooms: a front entry hall, formal parlor, library, back parlor, dining room, and kitchen.

The **FRONT ENTRY HALL** is a reminder that the High Victorian period was called "The Golden Age of Oak." The staircase is of golden oak with machine-carved spindles, which were at the time considered more modern, and therefore more desirable, than handcrafted ones. Also made of oak is the 46" high wainscotting, the fireplace mantel and the over mantel.

The walls and ceiling of the entry hall are covered with anaglypta, a brand name for a type of composition wall covering made of layers of paper pressed together, much like *papier-maché*, into designs. Lincrusta-Walton — a similar, but more durable, composition ornament — can be seen on the stairway dado. A derivative of linoleum, Lincrusta-Walton is made primarily of pressed linseed oil and fiber. Depending on how it is treated, it can be made to resemble embossed leather, carved wood, plasterwork or pressed tin. Damp-proof and easily cleaned, it was considered to be "...the most economical, durable and artistic wall covering on the market."

The **FORMAL PARLOR** is the most elaborately decorated room and was used for formal gatherings. The baseboards, window casings and fireplace mantel are all made of cherry wood. Architect William Lang used stained glass extensively in his designs, and the arched stained glass window in this room, as well as the two on the stairway landing, were locally made and are original to the house. The floors in this room and the library are made of hemlock but are painted or "grained" to look like oak. Woodwork on the second floor has also been grained.

The wallpaper in the formal parlor has been authentically reproduced. During the restoration of the formal parlor, curators discovered a fragment of the original wallpaper behind one of the radiators and were delighted to learn that it

The upstairs study was originally designed as a bedroom. The wallpaper was reproduced from a fragment found during restoration. *Photo by Roger Whitacre.*

Shortly after they bought the property, the Browns doubled the size of the carriage house. The original southern section stored the Browns' carriage and harnesses; the second floor serving as living quarters for the stable boy. The northern addition contained four stalls, a trough and hayloft. Later, it housed Maggie's electric car. *Photo by Roger Whitacre.*

was still being manufactured by an English firm.

The **LIBRARY** had originally been designed as a back parlor, but Maggie had built-in bookcases installed and used it as a library. The tobacco brown color of the walls is original.

The **BACK PARLOR**, which the architects originally designed as a library, was the family's less formal sitting area. It is now used as museum offices.

A highlight of the **DINING ROOM** is the unusual conservatory ceiling, the colors and design of which have been accurately reproduced from photographs and existing physical evidence. Also unique are the combed plaster walls. Among the original Brown furnishings featured in this room are the elegant punchbowl, the silver soup tureen and the carving set.

The dining room also features one of the house's four original fireplaces, which were merely aesthetic since the house was built with central heat.

The **KITCHEN/PANTRY AREA** was not photographed in Maggie's day (probably because it was too utilitarian) and, because it had been so extensively remodeled, was one of the greatest restoration challenges for Historic Denver curators.

The kitchen is a large, practical room — the requirements of primary concern being ventilation, light, cleanliness and convenience. The table was used for servants' meals and food preparation. The varnished cupboards have been reconstructed in their original locations. Kitchen utensils are typical of those in use between 1900 and 1910.

The butler's pantry, the area immediately entered from the dining room, was used as a storage area for dinnerware and glassware. The cook's pantry off the kitchen was used as a work area and for storing utensils and food staples. Also leading off the kitchen area is the back staircase which leads to the second floor, as well as to the third-floor servants' quarters. A 1904 newspaper account indicates that the Brown family household included a cook, two "second girls," a coachman and a stable boy. At other times, the staff included a housekeeper and a dressmaker.

The second floor contains a sunroom, which features an

The dining room shows the eclectic tastes of the Victorian era, featuring oriental rugs, animal heads, tapestries and hand-painted china. *Photo courtesy Denver Public Library, Western History Department.*

outdoor balcony, four bedrooms (which have been assigned names by the museum staff), a study and a bath.

The stained glass window in the **SUNROOM** is the only restored one in the house. It had been removed and was found, broken into pieces, in the basement. It was restored to its original design using as much of the original glass as possible.

HELEN'S ROOM, the front bedroom, was, according to 1920s correspondence, Maggie's favorite. It is one of three bedrooms which feature upholstered walls, a very popular and luxurious wall treatment of the early 20th century. The fabric-covered walls, which are soft to the touch, muffle sound and delight the eye with subtle pattern changes as light reflects off the brocaded surfaces. The blue tapestry fabric in Helen's room matches that on the elaborately carved four-poster bed, which is original to the house.

MOLLY'S ROOM is upholstered in dark green silk, and **J.J.'S ROOM**, the only bedroom with a fireplace, is finished in light green.

Maggie's parents lived with her until their deaths and the **TOBIN ROOM** in the southeast corner of the second floor is named in their honor. The modestly decorated room features mementoes of Maggie's earlier and simpler life, including two plaster vases and two oil paintings which she and J.J. received as wedding gifts.

The **STUDY** was originally designed as a bedroom. The striking, geometrically-designed wallpaper has been accurately reproduced from a fragment found during restoration.

The third floor was used primarily as servants' quarters. However, the Browns added the stairway which leads from the second to the third floor and newspaper accounts indicate the third floor was used occasionally as a ballroom.

The Molly Brown House Museum grounds have been restored according to Victorian taste with hollyhocks, lilacs, sweet william and peonies. The restoration even includes a small vegetable garden for Maggie's cook.

Inside and out, the Molly Brown House Museum has been so accurately restored that Maggie herself would feel right at home. It's a fitting tribute to one of Denver's most remarkable women.

Acknowledgements

This book was compiled from research that was done over a ten-year period by Molly Brown House Museum staff and volunteers. In particular, the author would like to thank Lyn Spenst, who has researched the Brown family for nearly ten years as both a volunteer and Molly Brown House Museum curator. The author has also drawn extensively on the resources of the Western History Department of the Denver Public Library and the Colorado Historical Society. The latter was invaluable in that it houses the Brown Family Papers, which were willed to the Colorado Historical Society by the estate of Lawrence P. Brown in 1957 and opened to the public in 1976.

Acknowledgement also goes to Roberta Hagood of Hannibal, Missouri, for all the research she so generously supplied on the Tobin family. The author is especially grateful to Historic Denver's Publications Committee, who conceived the idea for this book and whose help was essential in following that idea through the various writing, editing and publication stages. Committee members are: Sandra Dallas Atchison, Charles W. Cleworth, Gordon C. Jones, Margaret A. McKechnie and Thomas J. Noel. And, finally, special thanks go to Historic Denver Executive Director Elizabeth Schlosser, and Communications Director Elizabeth S. Downs for their assistance.

For those wishing to do more research on Margaret Tobin Brown, an annotated copy of this book is available through the offices of Historic Denver, Inc.

About the author

Like most people, Christine Whitacre first heard of Margaret Tobin Brown through stage and screen productions of *The Unsinkable Molly Brown.* Later, she learned more about Molly's life while serving as Historic Denver's Publications Director. A Chicago native who moved to Colorado in 1972, Whitacre is a graduate of the University of Illinois and has worked for Chicago's Field Museum and the Western States Arts Foundation in Denver. Whitacre is also the author of *The Restoration Resource Guide,* published by Historic Denver in 1981. She is married to Denver photographer Roger Whitacre and has two children, Emily and William.